Legislative branch
of the Government

Written by Julia Hargrove

Illustrated by Bron Smith

Teaching & Learning Company

1204 Buchanan St., P.O. Box 10
Carthage, IL 62321-0010

This book belongs to

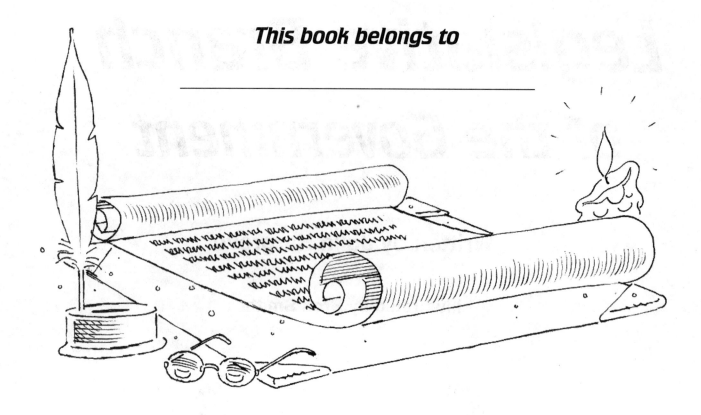

Cover photo courtesy of the Library of Congress

Copyright © 2000, Teaching & Learning Company

ISBN No. 1-57310-245-8

Printing No. 9876543

Teaching & Learning Company
1204 Buchanan St., P.O. Box 10
Carthage, IL 62321-0010

Table of Contents

Dear Teacher or Parent,

This book is one in a series by the Teaching & Learning Company on the three branches of the United States government. Together the three will show the powers of each branch, how they interact with one another in a system requiring separation of powers and how each branch is designed to prevent the other two branches from assuming too much power.

It is important that young people understand their national government because that government is working for them and for all citizens. However, it cannot do the best job possible without the participation of its citizens. Certainly we look to the government to solve many of our problems: to provide emergency relief after natural disasters, to defend us from foreign enemies, to make sure the food we eat is wholesome and the medicine we take is effective, to take care of us in our old age and to help provide money for schools for our young people. In return, we have our responsibilities, too. We must pay our taxes; vote in elections; be well-informed about candidates and national issues when we vote; let our representatives, senators and the President know our opinions about pending legislation and act as watchdogs when the government is not working for our best interests. One of the ways we can help young people to grow into responsible citizens is to help them understand how their government works.

This book about the Legislative Branch teaches students about congressional committees, lobbying and how a bill becomes a law. Students will write their own bills and hold a mock Congress to simulate the legislative process. Article I is also included to show how Congress was created and what its powers and duties are. I hope you find these materials useful in teaching your child or student.

Sincerely,

Julia

Julia Hargrove

Article I–Legislative Department

Section I. Congress

1) All legislative powers herein granted shall be vested in a Congress of the United States, which shall consist of a Senate and House of Representatives.

Section II. House of Representatives

1) The House of Representatives shall be composed of members chosen every second year by the people of the several States, and the electors in each State shall have the qualifications requisite for electors of the most numerous branch of the State Legislature.

2) No person shall be a Representative who shall not have attained to the age of twenty-five years, and been seven years a citizen of the United States, and who shall not, when elected, be an inhabitant of that State in which he shall be chosen.

3) Representatives and direct taxes shall be apportioned among the several States which may be included in this Union, according to their respective numbers. The actual enumeration shall be made within three years after the first meeting of the Congress of the United States, and within every subsequent term of 10 years, in such manner as they shall by law direct. The number of Representatives shall not exceed one for every thirty thousand, but each State shall have at least one Representative.

4) When vacancies happen in the representation from any State, the Executive authority thereof shall issue writs of election to fill such vacancies.

5) The House of Representatives shall choose their Speaker and other officers; and shall have the sole power of impeachment.

Section I. Congress

1) Congress will have all the lawmaking powers of the United States' national government. The Congress will have a Senate and a House of Representatives.

Section II. House of Representatives

1) Each state will elect its members to the House of Representatives every two years. Each state's electors must meet the same requirements for election as the requirements for members of the state's house of representatives.

2) Representatives must be at least 25 years old, a citizen of the United States for at least seven years and an inhabitant of the state from which he or she was elected.

3) The number of representatives and the amount of direct taxes for each state will be decided by the size of the population of each state. The actual count of the population (census) will begin within three years of the first meeting of Congress. Future census counts will be taken every 10 years and done as the law says. Each state will have one representative for every 30,000 people. Every state will have at least one representative.

4) If a senator or representative dies or is removed from office during the term, the governor of the state calls for an election to fill the office left open.

5) The House of Representatives chooses its own Speaker and other officers. Only the House has the power to impeach (bring charges against) senators, representatives, the President or a Supreme Court justice.

Article I–Legislative Department

Section III. Senate

Section III. Senate

1) The Senate of the United States shall be composed of two Senators from each State, for six years; and each Senator shall have one vote.

2) Immediately after they shall be assembled in consequence of the first election, they shall be divided as equally as may be into three classes. The seats of the Senators of the first class shall be vacated at the expiration of the second year, of the second class at the expiration of the fourth year, and of the third class at the expiration of the sixth year, so that one-third may be chosen every second year.

3) No person shall be a senator who shall not have attained to the age of thirty years, and been nine years a citizen of the United States, and who shall not, when elected, be an inhabitant of that State for which he shall be chosen.

4) The Vice President of the United States shall be President of the Senate, but shall have no vote, unless they be equally divided.

5) The Senate shall choose their other officers, and also a President Pro Tempore, in the absence of the Vice President, or when he shall exercise the office of President of the United States.

6) The Senate shall have the sole power to try all impeachments. When sitting for that purpose, they shall be on oath or affirmation. When the President of the United States is tried, the Chief Justice shall preside and no person shall be convicted without the concurrence of two-thirds of the members present.

Section III. Senate

1) The Senate is made up of two senators from each state. Senators hold office for six years. Each senator has one vote in the Senate.

2) Right after they took office in 1789, the first senators were divided into three groups. The first group served for two years, the second for four years and the third for six years. The reason for this was to create a system in which one-third of the senators are up for election every two years.

3) To be a senator, a person must be at least 30 years old, a citizen of the U.S. for at least nine years and a resident of the state from which he or she was elected.

4) The Vice President of the U.S. is the President of the Senate. He or she can only vote in the Senate if there is a tie in the voting.

5) The Senate chooses all of its other officers. One of those officers is the President Pro Tempore (temporary President), who serves when the Vice President is away or is acting as President of the U.S.

6) Only the Senate can hold impeachment trials. During such a trial, the senators take an oath. If the President is on trial, the Chief Justice of the Supreme Court runs the Senate and the trial. It takes a two-thirds vote (at least 67 senators) to convict in impeachment cases.

Article I–Legislative Department

7) Judgment in cases of impeachment shall not extend further than to removal from office, and disqualification to hold and enjoy any office of honor, trust, or profit under the United States; but the party convicted shall nevertheless be liable and subject to indictment, trial, judgment, and punishment, according to law.

7) The punishment for being found guilty in an impeachment case is being removed from office and prevented from running for any office in the future. After an impeachment trial, a person can still be tried, convicted and punished according to criminal or civil law.

Section IV. Both Houses

1) The times, places, and manner of holding elections for Senators and Representatives shall be prescribed in each State by the Legislature thereof; but the Congress may at any time by law make or alter such regulations, except as to the places of choosing Senators.

Section IV. Both Houses

1) The legislature of each state decides when, where and how its senators and representatives will be elected. The states can change their laws about these elections except for where senators are elected.

2) The Congress shall assemble at least once in every year, and such meeting shall be on the first Monday in December, unless they shall by law appoint a different day.

2) Congress must meet at least once a year beginning on the first Monday in December. Congress can pass a law changing the date they meet.

Section V. Each House Alone

1) Each house shall be the judge of the elections, returns, and qualifications of its own members, and a majority of each shall constitute a quorum to do business; but a smaller number may adjourn from day to day, and may be authorized to compel the attendance of absent members, in such manner, and under such penalties, as each house may provide.

Section V. Each House Alone

1) Each house judges the qualifications and votes of its own members. A quorum exists when a majority of the house's members is present. A smaller number of members may leave each day. The minority may also force other members to attend a session and punish them if they don't.

2) Each house may determine the rules of its proceedings, punish its members for disorderly behavior, and, with the concurrence of two-thirds, expel a member.

2) Each house makes its own rules of how it is run. Each house can punish members who misbehave and kick them out by a two-thirds vote.

3) Each house shall keep a journal of its proceedings, and from time to time publish the same, excepting such parts as may in their judgment require secrecy; and the yeas and nays of the members of either house on any question shall, at the desire of one-fifth of those present, be entered on the journal.

3) Each house keeps a record of what it does and publishes the record periodically. It doesn't have to reveal parts of the record that it wants to keep secret. A record of the yes and no votes on an issue will be written in the journal if one-fifth of the members want it to be done.

Article I–Legislative Department

4) Neither house, during the session of Congress, shall, without the consent of the other, adjourn for more than three days, nor to any other place than that in which the two houses shall be sitting.

4) Neither house can adjourn for more than three days without the other houses agreeing to it. They cannot adjourn to another place.

Section VI. Privileges and Restrictions

1) The Senators and Representatives shall receive a compensation for their services, to be ascertained by law, and paid out of the treasury of the United States. They shall in all cases, except treason, felony, and breach of the peace, be privileged from arrest during their attendance at the session of their respective houses, and in going to and returning from the same; and for any speech or debate in either house they shall not be questioned in any other place.

Section VI. Privileges and Restrictions

1) The Senators and Representatives will be paid. The amount of their salary is set by law and paid for out of the U.S. Treasury. They cannot be arrested while Congress is in session except for charges of treason, felony or breach of the peace. They cannot be arrested while going to or leaving a session of Congress. They cannot be questioned or arrested for what they say in a speech or debate.

2) No Senator or Representative shall, during the time for which he was elected, be appointed to any civil office under the authority of the United States, which shall have been created, or the emoluments whereof shall have been increased, during such time; and no person holding any office under the United States shall be a member of either house during his continuance in office.

2) A senator or representative cannot take an office that was created or whose salary was raised during his term in office. No person already holding a job in the federal government can be a member of either house as long as he still holds the first job.

SORRY, SNIDLEY! TRY AGAIN AFTER YOU'VE LOST THE NEXT ELECTION.

Name _____

The Two Houses of Congress

1. Fill in the chart below about representatives' and senators' terms in office and the qualifications required to be elected to office.

Office	Term in Office	Age Qualification	Citizenship Qualification	Residence Qualification
Representative				
Senator				

2. Below are several things the houses of Congress can do. Decide which house(s) can do these things and choose one of the following answers to write in the blank beside the action:
   a. House of Representatives only   b. Senate only   c. both houses   d. neither house

_____ a. The state legislature decides when, where and how the elections for this house of Congress will be held.

_____ b. This house can bring impeachment charges against federal office holders.

_____ c. This house can hold trials for office holders who have been impeached.

_____ d. Only one-third of the members of this house are up for election during any national election year.

_____ e. This house elects a Speaker who runs its meetings.

_____ f. This house can punish its own members for misbehavior.

_____ g. No member of this house can be arrested for any crime except treason, felony or breach of the peace.

_____ h. The number of people elected by a state to this house is based on the size of the state's population.

_____ i. This house must keep a journal that tells what has happened in the house.

_____ j. This house cannot adjourn (leave) without the consent of the other house.

Article I, Section VII– Methods of Passing Laws

1) All bills for raising revenue shall originate in the House of Representatives, but the Senate may propose or concur with amendments as on other bills.

2) Every bill which shall have passed the House of Representatives and the Senate shall, before it becomes a law, be presented to the President of the United States; if he approves he shall sign it, but if not he shall return it with his objections to that house in which it shall have originated, who shall enter the objections at large on their journal, and proceed to reconsider it. If after such reconsideration two-thirds of that shall agree to pass the bill, it shall be sent together with the objections, to the other house, by which it shall likewise be reconsidered, and, if approved by two-thirds of that house, it shall become a law. But in all such cases the votes of both houses shall be determined by yeas and nays, and the names of the persons voting for and against the bill shall be entered on the journal of each house respectively. If any bill shall not be returned by the President within ten days (Sundays excepted) after it shall have been presented to him, the same shall be a law, in like manner as if he had signed it, unless the Congress by their adjournment prevent its return, in which case it shall not be law.

3) Every order, resolution, or vote to which the concurrence of the Senate and House of Representatives may be necessary (except on a question of adjournment) shall be presented to the President of the United States, and before the same shall take effect, shall be approved by him, or, being disapproved by him, shall be repassed by two-thirds of the Senate and House of Representatives, according to the rules and limitations prescribed in the case of a bill.

1) All taxes that create or increase taxes must begin in the House of Representatives. The Senate can suggest or agree to amendments to tax bills.

2) Every bill that passes the House and the Senate goes to the President before it becomes law. If he agrees with the bill, he signs it into law. If he doesn't agree, he returns it to the house where it began with a list of the reasons why he doesn't agree. The house enters his objections in its journal and discusses the bill again. If two-thirds of this house passes the bill, it goes to the other house along with the President's reasons against the bill. The second house discusses the bill again. If that house also passes the bill by a two-thirds note, the bill becomes a law. In this process, a roll call vote is held in each house. The name of the person and the way he or she voted is recorded in each house's journal. If the President doesn't send a bill back to one of the houses within 10 days after it is sent to him, the bill automatically becomes a law (even if the President doesn't sign it). The only exception is if Congress adjourns before the bill is returned.

3) Every order, resolution or vote that both the House and Senate have to agree on must go to the President also for his approval. (The exception is a vote to end a session.) If the President doesn't approve of the action, but it is repassed by a two-thirds vote in both houses, it becomes legal the same way a bill would be a law.

Methods of Passing Laws

An idea for a law can be introduced into either the House of Representatives or the Senate. Before it becomes a law, the idea is called a bill. The Clerk of the House reads the bill to the house, assigns it a number (such as HR 128 or S 385) and has it printed. The Speaker of the House or the President Pro Tempore of the Senate assigns the bill to a committee. The committee studies each bill before it goes before the whole house. Committees are necessary because there are too many bills introduced each year for every member of Congress to read all of them. Members of the committee study the bill, hold hearings on it and call witnesses to testify about the good and bad effects if the bill becomes a law. The committee has the power to kill a bill (defeat it), pigeonhole it (put it aside for a long time), amend (change) it or recommend the passage of the bill and send it to the entire house. The clerk reads the bill to the house a second time after which the house debates whether the bill should be passed or not. Members can amend the bill, add riders (clauses completely unrelated to the bill itself) or pass the bill as written.

When the bill passes the house where it was introduced, it goes to the other house where it goes through the same process of committee hearings and vote by the house. If the bill is rejected by either house, it does not become law. If it is passed by both houses but there are differences between the House bill and the Senate bill, the bill goes to a joint committee of both houses where the differences are ironed out.

After the bill passes both houses, it must be sent to the President for his approval. The President can do one of four things with the bill. He can (1) sign it, (2) keep it for more than 10 days without signing it or vetoing it, (3) keep it for 10 days during which the Congress adjourns or (4) veto it.

(1) If the President signs a bill within the 10-day period, it becomes a law.

(2) If the President keeps a bill for more than 10 days without signing it or vetoing it, the bill automatically becomes a law. This is a way the President can show that he disagrees with the bill even though he knows that it must become law for the good of the citizens or for political reasons.

(3) In rare situations, the President holds the bill without signing it, but during the 10-day waiting period, the Congress ends its session. This is called a pocket veto. The bill does not become a law.

(4) If the President vetoes a bill, he defeats it. A veto is the refusal of a President to sign a bill into law. If this happens, the President must send the bill back to the house of Congress where it began with a list of the reasons why he doesn't like the bill.

Even if the President vetoes a bill, it can still become a law if Congress is very determined. When one of the houses gets the bill back, its members can discuss it again. The members of that house can either rewrite the bill to take care of the President's objections and pass the new version, or it can repass the original bill by a two-thirds vote. If the original version of the bill passes the first house, it is then sent to the other one where the same process occurs. A roll call vote must be taken in each house to prove that the two-thirds majority was reached. In such a vote, the name of each member of the house is called, he or she votes "yea" or "nay," and the name and vote are recorded in the house journal. If both houses repass the bill by a two-thirds majority, it automatically becomes a law without the President's signature.

Methods of Passing Laws Outline

On the left is the outline form to use with this exercise. On the right are phrases that explain the steps a bill must go through to become a law. All of the steps will fit exactly into the outline. Begin with the main headings of the outline and fill in the details afterwards. Refer to the information on pages 10-11 to help with the outline.

I. A bill is introduced into one of the houses.   Congress votes to override President's veto.

    A.   Bill is read by the Clerk of the House.   President keeps the bill for 10 days without signing it.

    B. _____   Bill goes to other house to be voted on.

    C. _____   Bill goes to conference committee.

    D. _____   First house passes the bill.

    E. _____   President signs the bill into law.

II. _____   House debates the bill.

    A. _____   President vetoes the bill.

    B. _____   Bill is sent to committee.

III. _____   Bill is sent to President to sign.

    A. _____   Second house passes the bill.

    B. _____   Pocket veto occurs.

    C. _____   Committee sends bill to whole house.

    D. _____   President returns the vetoed bill to Congress.

IV. _____   Congress cannot get two-thirds vote to override veto.

    A. _____

    B. _____

12

Name _____

Mock Congress Rules

Purpose: To give students a direct experience in how Congress works.

1. Divide the class into groups of three or four students. These groups will play two roles: they will work to write a bill, and they will become committees that review bills.

2. Assign political parties to the groups or let them decide what party they represent.

3. Each group will nominate a classmate for Speaker of the House and for Clerk. The whole class will vote on the Speaker and the Clerk. Each group also selects its Chairperson.

4. Students do research and write their bills.

5. The documents go to the committee. (It might be a good idea for each bill to be submitted anonymously to prevent class rivalries and personality conflicts.)

6. Members of the committee read and debate the bill. They can approve the bill as written, amend the bill or kill the bill. If they decide to kill the bill, the group must provide written reasons for their action.

7. The bill's sponsors should have the opportunity to make changes to their bill and resubmit it to the committee if they want.

8. The approved bills go before the whole House. The sponsors should provide multiple, typed copies of their bill for all members to read. The Clerk of the House also reads the bill.

9. Members of the House debate the bills. Teacher sets limits on length of each debate. (Teacher might also take the opportunity to introduce some elements of Parliamentary Procedure.) House votes on each bill. Bills that pass might earn extra credit.

Time Table

First Day

Teacher assigns groups, groups decide on topic of their bill, groups decide what research they need to find and break up the research topics among members of the group.

Second Day

Students research their topics and hand in their notes at the end of the class period. (This could take two days depending on the success of the research efforts.)

Third Day

Students write their bills in their groups. (This might take two days.)

Fourth Day

Student groups meet as committees and review the bills.

Fifth Day

Students meet as the House of Representatives and vote on the proposed bills.

99th Congress
2D Session

H.R. 3298

To protect the rights of victims of child abuse.

IN THE HOUSE OF REPRESENTATIVES

September 12, 1985

Mr. Kemp (for himself, Mr. Stenholm, Mr. Siljander, Mr. Hendon, Mr. Weber

Mr. Dornan of California, Mr. Eckert of New York, Mr. Hiler, Mr. Smith of New Jersey,

and Mr. English) introduced the following bill;

which was referred to the Committee on the Judiciary.

January 22, 1986

Additional sponsors: Mr. Hammerschmidt, Mr. Kramer, Mr. Fields,

Mr. Bartlett, Mr. Rinaldo, Mr. Pashayan, Mr. Schaefer, Mr. Livingston,

Mrs. Lloyd, and Mr. Thomas of Georgia.

A Bill

To protect the rights of victims of child abuse.

1   *Be it enacted by the Senate and House of Representa-*

2   *tives of the United States of America in Congress assembled,*

3   SECTION I. SHORT TITLE.

4   This Act may be cited as the "Child Abuse Victims

5   Rights Act of 1985."

6   SECTION II. FINDINGS.

7   The Congress finds that—

Name _____

How to Write a Bill

Below is a list with explanations of the different parts of a bill. You will use these explanations to write your own bill on the next two pages.

1. At the top of the bill is the number that is assigned to a bill when it is introduced. The number begins with either S (for Senate) or HR (for House of Representatives) showing which house started the bill. The number that comes after the letters shows the number of bills introduced up to that point.

2. The purpose of the bill comes next. "To build a dam in Colorado on the Arkansas River" is an example.

3. The name of the house where the bill began is written next. "In the House of Representatives" or "In the Senate" are the two choices.

4. Below the name of the house is the date the bill was introduced and a list of the backers who support the bill.

5. The words *A Bill* and the purpose of the bill appear below the sponsors. An example of the purpose would be "To build a dam in Colorado on the Arkansas River."

6. Each bill begins with these exact words: *Be it enacted by the Senate and the House of Representatives of the United States of America in Congress assembled.*

7. Each line of the bill is numbered for quick reference when discussing the bill. Each page of the bill is numbered separately beginning with 1 and ending at about 25.

8. Section I of the bill is its short title. "This bill can be called the 'Arkansas River Dam Bill of (year).' "

9. Section II contains the findings that explain the reason for the bill. This would be several paragraphs about the research into the problem and explanations of why the bill is valuable.

10. Succeeding sections are the bill itself, telling what must be done if the bill is passed.

11. One section might name the government officer who has to carry out the law and how the bill will be carried out. For example, "The Secretary of the Interior will oversee the purchase of land in the Arkansas River Valley where the dam will be built."

12. The final section describes the penalty for breaking the law. For example, "If the construction company does not finish the dam by (a certain date), it will be fined $1000 for every day the work is not done."

Name _____

Write Your Own Bill

(Bill number)

(Purpose of bill)

(House where bill begins)

(Date bill introduced)

(List of sponsors)

A Bill

(Purpose of bill again)

1   *Be it enacted by the Senate and House of Representatives of the United States of*

2   *America in Congress assembled,*

3   SECTION I. SHORT TITLE.

SECTION II. FINDINGS.

Write Your Own Bill

SECTION III. (Actual bill)

SECTION IV. (Who will carry out the bill and how it will be carried out)

SECTION V. (Penalties)

Name _____

Article I, Section VIII– Powers Granted to Congress

The Congress shall have the power

1) To lay and collect taxes, duties*, imports and excises*, to pay the debts and provide for the common defense and general welfare of the United States; but all duties, imposts, and excises shall be uniform throughout the United States.

2) To borrow money on the credit of the United States;

3) To regulate commerce* with foreign nations, and among the several states, and with the Indian tribes;

4) To establish a uniform rule of naturalization,* and uniform laws on the subject of bankruptcies throughout the United States;

5) To coin money, regulate the value thereof, and of foreign coin, and fix the standard of weights and measures;

6) To provide for the punishment of counterfeiting* the securities and current coin of the United States;

Congress has the power to do these things.

1) It can pass tax laws and gather taxes such as taxes on foreign goods and goods made in the U.S. It can pay the debts of the U.S., protect the country with an army and navy and take care of the well-being of the nation. All national taxes must be the same within the U.S.

2) It can borrow money.

3) It can make laws about trade with foreign countries, trade among the states of the U.S. and trade with Indian tribes.

4) It can make laws about how immigrants become citizens of the U.S. It can make laws about people and businesses that lose all their money.

5) It can make coins and print paper money. It can decide the value of U.S. and foreign money in our country. It sets the same size for weights (such as a pound) and measures (such as a foot) throughout the U.S.

6) It decides what the punishment is for making false coins and paper money.

---

* **duties or imposts:** taxes put on goods that come into or go out of the country.

* **excise tax:** a tax put on luxury items (furs and jewelry) made inside this country.

* **commerce:** trade with foreign countries.

* **naturalization:** a legal process that makes a foreign-born person a citizen of the U.S.

* **counterfeiting:** making or passing fake money.

7)   To establish post offices and post roads.

7)   It can create offices for delivering the mail and build roads where the mail travels.

8)   To promote the progress of science and useful arts, by securing for limited times to authors and inventors the exclusive right to their respective writings and discoveries;

8)   It can grant copyrights* on written work and patents* on inventions to insure that authors and inventors get the money they deserve for their ideas.

9)   To constitute tribunals* inferior to the Supreme Court;

9)   It can create national courts that have more power than state courts but less power than the Supreme Court.

10)   To define and punish piracies* and felonies committed on the high seas and offences against the law of nations;

10)   It can define what are piracies and serious crimes on the seas. It can define what acts break international laws.

11)   To declare war, grant letters of marque and reprisal*, and make rules concerning captures on land and water;

11)   It can declare war. It can grant special papers that give private U.S. ships the right to capture foreign ships. It can make rules about U.S. armies and navies capturing enemies.

12)   To raise and support armies, but no appropriation* of money to that use shall be for a longer term than two years.

12)   It can create armies and give money to support them. No bill by Congress to provide money for the army can last more than two years.

13)   To provide and maintain a navy;

13)   It can create a navy and give money to support it.

14)   To make rules for the government and regulation of the land and naval forces;

14)   It can make rules that tell how the national government, the army and the navy should be run.

* **copyright:** right of an author to have sole control over his work for a number of years.

* **patent:** right of an inventor to have complete control over her work for a certain time.

* **tribunal:** a court of justice.

* **piracy:** robbery of ships on the oceans.

* **marque and reprisal:** official papers granting private ships the right to capture foreign ships during war.

* **appropriation:** money set aside by Congress for a specific use.

Article I, Section VIII– Powers Granted to Congress

15) To provide for calling forth the militia* to execute the laws of the Union, suppress insurrections*, and repel invasions;

16) To provide for organizing, arming, and disciplining the militia, and for governing such part of them as may be employed in the service of the United States, reserving to the States respectively, the appointment of the officers, and the authority of training the militia according to the discipline prescribed by Congress;

17) To exercise exclusive legislation, in all cases whatsoever, over such district (not exceeding ten miles square) as may, by cession of particular States, and the acceptance of Congress, become the seat of the government of the United States; and to exercise like authority over all places purchased by the consent of the Legislature of the State in which the same shall be, for the erection of forts, magazines*, arsenals*, dock-yards, and other needful buildings; and

18) To make all laws which shall be necessary and proper for carrying into execution the foregoing powers, and all other powers vested by this Constitution in the government of the United States, or in any department or officer thereof*.

15) It can make rules for calling up state troops in order to enforce the laws, put down rebellions and fight off foreign attacks on the U.S.

16) It can organize, arm and discipline the militia. It runs the part of the militia that is serving the national government (rather than the states). The states keep the power to appoint the militia's officers and to supervise training, but they follow rules about the militia passed by Congress.

17) Once the states and the Congress decide on what 10-square-mile piece of land will be the capital of the nation, Congress will make the laws for that city. Congress can also make laws for lands it buys from the states to build forts, weapon storage areas, ship-building docks and other necessary buildings.

18) It can make all laws that are necessary (and constitutional) for carrying out the above powers and all other powers given to the U.S. government by the Constitution.

* **militia:** any army of private citizens (not professional soldiers) that is only called to serve during a time of emergency.

* **insurrection:** an uprising against the established government of a nation.

* **magazines:** a place (within a larger structure) where ammunition and explosives are stored.

* **arsenal:** a place for storing weapons.

* **elastic clause:** Clause 18 is known as the "necessary and proper" or "elastic" clause because it allows Congress to expand its powers to cover things not written into the Constitution.

20

Powers of Congress Worksheet

Below are examples of actions Congress has taken. For each example, write below it the power from Article I, Section VIII that allowed Congress to do what it did.

1. The U.S. mints are coining five new quarters each year with designs to symbolize each of the 50 states. They have also created a new dollar coin with a picture of Sacajawea on it to replace the Susan B. Anthony dollar.

   Power: _____

2. Congress passed the Gold Standard Act in 1900. It said that paper money could be freely traded for gold from the U.S. government.

   Power: _____

3. In the 1920s, Congress passed the Hawley-Smoot Tariff, which placed very high taxes on foreign goods coming into the United States.

   Power: _____

4. Congress has created federal courts below the Supreme Court in power such as the United States Court of Appeals, the U.S. Tax Court and the U.S. Claims Court.

   Power: _____

5. In 1967, the Senate approved the appointments of a mayor-commissioner and nine members of a council established to govern the city of Washington, D.C.

   Power: _____

6. On December 8, 1941, President Franklin Roosevelt asked a special session of Congress to declare war on Japan because of the Japanese bombing of Pearl Harbor.

   Power: _____

7. During the American Revolution, Congress granted over 1000 privately owned, armed ships (privateers) the right to attack and capture British trading ships.

   Power: _____

8. During World War II, the federal government urged citizens to buy U.S. savings bonds in order to raise money to fight against Germany, Japan and Italy.

   Power: _____

Name _____

The Elastic Clause— Stretching the Powers of Congress

The elastic clause is found in Section VIII, Clause 18, which gives Congress the ability "to make all laws which shall be necessary and proper" for carrying out its powers. The Constitution could not have listed everything Congress needs to do to run a nation, so it outlined Congress's powers in broad terms and left the details for later.

Alexander Hamilton, the first Secretary of the Treasury, used the elastic clause to propose the Bank of the United States. Congress has the power to collect taxes and to borrow money, but the Constitution does not mention a power to create a banking system. However, Hamilton persuaded Congress that a national bank was necessary for organizing the collection of taxes and issuing securities for money it borrows. Congress created a national bank because it was "necessary and proper" to help them carry out their other powers.

Below are several examples of things Congress has done under the power of the elastic clause. In each case, the law or action was based on expanding one of the basic powers. Determine which original power was expanded and write that power in the space provided. Some powers may be used more than once.

1. In the 1950s, the federal government provided money for building a large system of highways across the United States.

   Power: _____

2. Congress passed the Interstate Commerce Act in 1887, the Elkins Act in 1903 and the Hepburn Act of 1906 to stop the worst abuses that interstate railroads were inflicting upon their customers through the prices they charged.

   Power: _____

3. The Sherman Anti-Trust Act of 1890 tried to regulate business monopolies that stopped trade by taking over large portions of a business or industry.

   Power: _____

4. During the Great Depression, Congress passed the Social Security Act of 1935. Two of its ideas were unemployment insurance for those out of work and payments to older citizens of $10 to $85 per month.

   Power: _____

5. After the Soviet Union put the first man-made satellite in orbit around the Earth in 1957, Congress passed the National Defense and Education Act. The Act provided money for needy students to study sciences and language in college.

   Power: _____

Name _____

Article I, Section IX–Powers Forbidden to the Federal Government

1) The migration or importation* of such persons as any of the States now existing shall think proper to admit, shall not be prohibited by the Congress prior to the year one thousand eight hundred and eight, but a tax or duty may be imposed on such importation, not exceeding ten dollars for each person.

1) Congress could not prevent states from importing slaves into the U.S. until 1808. Congress could place a tax on imported slaves, but the tax could not be more than $10 per slave. (This no longer applied after 1808.)

2) The privilege of the writ of *habeas corpus** shall not be suspended, unless when in cases of rebellion or invasion the public safety may require it.

2) A person cannot be held in jail with little or no evidence against him, except at times of revolution or invasion by an enemy when the safety of the public might require that certain people be jailed.

3) No bill of attainder* or *ex post facto* law* shall be passed.

3) Congress cannot pass a law that says a person is guilty of a crime and also punishes that person. It also cannot pass a law that makes past actions illegal when they were legal at the time they occurred.

4) No capitation* or other direct tax shall be laid, unless in proportion to the census or enumeration* therein before directed to be taken.

4) No direct tax on each individual person can be passed by Congress, except if it is based on the census (a count of the population).

* **migration or importation:** allowing or bringing foreign people into the country.

* **writ of *habeas corpus*:** a court order that requires that a person be brought from jail to a courtroom to see if there is enough evidence to charge that person with a crime. If there is not enough evidence, that person must be released.

* **bill of attainder:** a law that finds a person guilty of a crime and decides punishment without a trial.

* **ex *post facto* law:** a law that makes a past action illegal even though it was legal at the time it happened.

* **capitation tax:** a tax or fee of so much per head (or person).

* **enumeration (or census):** a count of the number of people in a country.

Article I, Section IX – Powers Forbidden to the Federal Government

5) No tax or duty shall be laid on articles exported from any state.

6) No preference shall be given by any regulation of commerce* or revenue* to the ports of one State over those of another; nor shall vessels bound to, or from, one State, be obliged to enter, clear, or pay duties in another.

7) No money shall be drawn from the treasury, but in consequence of appropriations* made by law; and a regular statement and account of the receipts* and expenditures* of all public money shall be published from time to time.

8) No title of nobility* shall be granted by the United States; and no person holding any office of profit or trust under them shall, without the consent of the Congress, accept of any present, emolument*, office, or title, of any kind whatever, from any king, prince, or foreign state.

5) Congress cannot put a tax on any product shipped out of any state.

6) Congress cannot make any law that favors one state's seaports over other states' ports. Ships from one state cannot be required to go through other states' ports or to pay taxes in another state's ports.

7) The federal treasury will not pay out any money unless Congress passes an appropriations law setting aside that money for special use. Periodically, Congress will publish a statement showing the income and payments of all public money.

8) The U.S. government cannot give people titles of nobility (such as "duke" or "prince"). No person who works for the federal government can accept any special favors (such as presents, money, titles, or jobs) from any foreign country or ruler.

* **commerce:** trade within a country or with a foreign country.

* **revenue:** a nation's income from taxes, duties, licenses, fees, etc.

* **appropriation:** money set aside by Congress for a specific purpose (such as paying the wages of soldiers).

* **receipt:** a written statement proving that goods or money has been received by the person or business for which it was intended.

* **expenditures:** money paid out to buy things or settle a debt.

* **title of nobility:** a title that shows royalty or members of the upper class; examples are "prince," "duke," "countess," "lady," "sir."

* **emolument:** a payment received for work done.

Name _____

Article I, Section X–
Powers Forbidden to the States

1) No State shall enter into any treaty, alliance, or confederation*; grant letters of marque and reprisal*; coin money, emit bills of credit; make anything but gold and silver coins a tender* in payments of debts; pass any bill of attainder, *ex post facto* law, or law impairing the obligation of contracts*; or grant any title of nobility.

1) States cannot make any treaty with or join up as a part of a foreign country. They cannot give private ships the right to capture foreign trading ships, mint money of their own, give out bills of credit on national money, or make anything but gold or silver legal payment for debts. They cannot pass laws that find people guilty without a trial or that make past actions illegal (when they were legal at the time they happened).

2) No State shall, without the consent of the Congress, lay any imposts or duties* on imports or exports, except what may be absolutely necessary for executing its inspection laws; and the net produce of all duties and imposts, laid by any State on imports and exports, shall be for the use of the Treasury of the United States; and all such laws shall be subject to the revision and control of the Congress.

2) Without the approval of Congress, no state can put taxes on imports or exports except as part of its inspection laws. All money the states collect as taxes on imports and exports must be put in the national treasury. All laws that put taxes on imports and exports are controlled by and can be changed by Congress.

3) No State shall, without the consent of Congress, lay any duty on tonnage*, keep troops or ships of war in time of peace, enter into any agreement or compact with another State, or with a foreign power, or engage in war, unless actually invaded, or in such imminent danger as will not admit of delay.

3) Unless Congress agrees, states cannot tax ships by weight of cargo, keep armies or navies in times of peace, or make any agreement with another U.S. state or foreign power. They can fight a war only if they are being invaded or are in great danger.

* **confederation:** a loose union of states or nations.

* **letters of marque and reprisal:** official papers that allow a private ship to capture ships or other nations during time of war.

* **tender (or legal tender):** something that is accepted by the government as legal to use for the payment of debt. Paper money, coins, gold and silver are legal tender.

* **contract:** a written agreement between two people to do something. Many contracts provide a product or service from one side in return for money from the other side.

* **impost or duty:** a tax on goods brought into or sent out of a country.

* **tonnage:** a tax placed on ships according to the weight (in tons) of the goods it carries.

25

Name _____

Powers Forbidden to the Federal Government or to the States

Below is a list of powers that either the federal government or the state government or both cannot use. Write each of the powers under the correct heading. If a power goes under the Powers Forbidden to Both Federal and State Governments, write it only under that heading.

coin money
pass bills of attainder
emit bills of credit
pass ex *post facto* laws
grant titles of nobility
keep armies and navies during peace
tax exports

grant letters of marque and reprisal
fight a war
suspend a writ of *habeas corpus*
make laws that harm contracts

pay out money without appropriations law
tax imports or exports except for inspections
enter foreign treaty or alliance
make a treaty or alliance with a state

Powers Forbidden to Federal Government	Powers Forbidden to the States

Powers Forbidden to Both Federal and State Governments

TLC10245 Copyright © Teaching & Learning Company, Carthage, IL 62321-0010

Name _____

Thinking Skills: Classifying Vocabulary Words

Use the definitions on each page in this unit for the classification exercise. Below are several categories that are general terms for groups of vocabulary words. In the spaces provided, write the words that fit the category. Some vocabulary terms may be used more than once because some categories overlap.

A.   Unfair Laws

    1. _____

    2. _____

B.   Types of Taxes

    1. _____

    2. _____

    3. _____

C.   Words That Name Income (Not Taxes) for a Person or Country

    1. _____

    2. _____

D.   Words About Business or Trading Goods

    1. _____

    2. _____

    3. _____

    4. _____

E.   Things That Require Counting People

    1. _____

    2. _____

Separation of Powers and Checks and Balances

One of the most important concepts in the way the federal government works is called separation of powers. This means that each of the three branches has different powers and responsibilities in running the government. The purpose of separation of powers is to prevent any one leader or branch of government from taking over the whole power of government. The power is divided among the branches in this way: the legislative branch (Congress) makes the laws, the executive branch (President) carries out the laws and the judicial branch (Supreme Court) interprets the laws.

To say that Congress makes the laws means that senators and representatives pass legislation that makes certain ideas the law of the land. For instance, in the 1930s Congress passed the Social Security Act that made the idea of government retirement payments to older people into a law. The first payments were $10 to $85 per month.

What is meant by the President's power to carry out the laws is that the executive is the law enforcement branch. The President has the power to use the military, the FBI and other agencies to make people obey the laws and to arrest people who don't obey them. One example is from the 1950s when the Supreme Court ordered that all public schools be integrated. When Central High School in Little Rock, Arkansas, refused to allow blacks to attend, President Eisenhower sent troops to make the people integrate their school. He carried out the law.

The Supreme Court decides what the law means. The Court does this through trials in which the meaning of the law is argued by the prosecution and the defense. The Court declared the Judiciary Act of 1789 unconstitutional; they interpreted the meaning of the law and said it went against what the Constitution said was legal.

28

Separation of Powers

For each of the situations described below, decide whether it shows separation of powers in the federal government or not. If it is an example of the federal separation of powers, write *yes* in the space provided. If not, write *no*.

_____ 1. If a representative dies or is removed from office, the governor of the state where the representative was elected declares a new election to vote for a replacement.

_____ 2. The President and his Office of Management and Budget write the federal budget, but it goes to Congress to be studied, amended and approved.

_____ 3. Congress has the power to declare war, but the President, as commander in chief, has the power to order troops to foreign countries.

_____ 4. Congress has the "power of purse." That means that in some cases, if Congress disagrees with a presidential action, it can refuse to pass a law providing the money for that action.

_____ 5. The members of the House of Representatives serve two-year terms, while the senators serve six-year terms.

_____ 6. The House and Senate both have to publish journals telling what they have done so that the people will know whether their government is doing what they want.

_____ 7. Congress has the power to create federal courts below the Supreme Court and to decide the duties of those courts.

_____ 8. Only the House of Representatives can begin a bill that creates or raises taxes, but the Senate can suggest amendments to the bill.

_____ 9. The President cannot arrest or question members of Congress for things they might say in speeches or debates in the House of Representatives or the Senate.

_____ 10. Neither senators nor representatives can hold any other federal office while they are serving their terms in Congress.

_____ 11. The Vice President of the U.S. serves as the President of the Senate.

Checks and Balances

The idea of checks and balances works with separation of powers to prevent a single leader or any one of the branches from taking total control of the federal government. Checks and balances are written into the Constitution. They give each branch some powers over the other two branches so that each can help check or prevent the other two from gaining all the power in the government. For instance, the President can appoint Supreme Court justices, but the Senate has the power to confirm or reject the President's appointments. That way, the President cannot control the Supreme Court by appointing his friends and making the Court automatically support anything he wants to do. Below are examples of checks that each branch has over the other two.

A. Executive Branch (President)
1. He appoints Supreme Court justices.
2. He can veto laws passed by Congress.
3. He is commander in chief of the military and can move troops to danger spots throughout the world.
4. He has the power to grant pardons and reprieves and to commute sentences of criminals.

B. Legislative Branch (Congress)
1. The Senate confirms the appointments of Supreme Court justices.
2. Congress can overturn a presidential veto by a two-thirds vote of both houses.
3. The Senate ratifies treaties made by the President or his ambassadors.
4. The Senate confirms appointments of ambassadors and other foreign representatives recommended by the President.
5. The House of Representatives impeaches the President; the Senate tries the President on impeachment charges.
6. Only Congress can declare war.
7. Only Congress can appropriate money to carry out laws or to pay for the President's movement of military troops overseas.

C. Judicial Branch (Supreme Court)
1. The Supreme Court can declare congressional laws and Executive Orders unconstitutional.
2. The Chief Justice of the Supreme Court presides over an impeachment trial of a President.

30

Name _____

Checks and Balances

These questions are based on the information about checks and balances. If the situation described shows one of the checks that Congress has (even if Congress agrees to the action), write *yes* in the blank provided. If it is not, write *no*.

_____ 1. Congress, dominated by the Radical Republicans, passed the Civil Rights Bill in March 1866. Andrew Johnson vetoed the bill, but in April Congress overrode the President's veto and voted the bill into law.

_____ 2. President Clinton was impeached by the House of Representatives in 1998 and tried on the impeachment charges by the Senate in 1998-99. He was acquitted.

_____ 3. Neither the Senate nor the House of Representatives can adjourn a session without consent of the other house.

_____ 4. In the 1930s, President Roosevelt wanted to increase the number of justices on the Supreme Court so that his New Deal policies would not be declared unconstitutional. The Senate defeated a bill that would have given Roosevelt his way.

_____ 5. In 1964, relatively early in the Vietnam War, Congress passed the Tonkin Gulf Resolution that gave President Johnson almost all of the war-making powers that the Constitution gave to Congress.

_____ 6. In the 1970s after the Vietnam War, Congress passed the War Powers Act that limited the amount of time the President could send troops into a foreign country without the consent of Congress.

_____ 7. After a long and sometimes bitter debate in the Senate, that house confirmed the President's appointment of Clarence Thomas to the Supreme Court.

_____ 8. Amendment 16 had to be ratified by the states before the federal government could make people pay income taxes.

_____ 9. Henry Cabot Lodge worked very hard to stop the Senate from ratifying the Treaty of Versailles that President Wilson had helped to write after World War I.

_____ 10. President Wilson tried to gain public favor for the Treaty of Versailles and the League of Nations by making speeches to citizens throughout the United States.

_____ 11. Electors choose the President after the popular election is held. No senator or representative can serve as an elector.

_____ 12. Once a year the President appears before a joint session of Congress to make a speech on the state of the United States and to suggest ideas for laws that he would like to have Congress pass.

Officers of the Senate and House of Representatives

Below are the names of congressional officers, their jobs and their level of importance in each house. As you read, mark key words that tell you where each officer goes on the chart on the following page. The first office is done for you.

1. The <u>House of Representatives</u> has a **Speaker** who is the <u>most important officer</u> in that house. The majority party—the political party with the most members in the House—elects the Speaker. He or she holds great power: the ability to influence the order of business in the House and the power to call representatives who want to speak.

2. Both political parties have **party whips**, who are important but of lower rank than the floor leaders. Party whips have the job of persuading members to vote for bills sponsored by their own political party. He or she can also try to persuade people of the opposite party to vote for the bill.

3. The most important officer in the Senate is the Vice President of the United States. He or she is the **President of the Senate** and runs the business of the Senate. The Vice President cannot vote on bills unless there is a tie among the senators.

4. The Senate also has **party whips** who have the same duties and rank as those in the House.

5. The floor leader has the very important job of guiding his or her party's bills through Congress so that they get passed. The **majority leader** does this for the party with the most members, and the **minority leader** does the same job for the party with the fewest members. These leaders rank above the party whips but are less powerful than the Speaker or President *Pro Tempore*.

6. When the Vice President of the U.S. is away from his job in the Senate, the **President *Pro Tempore*** runs the Senate. The members of the Senate elect this officer, but the custom is to elect the longest-serving member of the majority party to do the job. Because the Vice President is frequently away on other business, the President *Pro Tempore* is the one who runs the Senate's business and, therefore, is second to the Vice President in importance.

7. The Senate also has a **majority leader** and a **minority leader** to push their party's bills through Congress. They hold the same rank as the House majority and minority leaders, but they are less important than the President *Pro Tempore* in their house.

8. Other senators and representatives have roles as heads of committees. The **head of a committee** like the Ways and Means Committee in the Senate is among the most powerful committee leaders but less important than leaders responsible for getting bills passed through Congress.

Name _____

Ranking Congressional Officers

Use the clues you have underlined on the previous page to fill in the chart below from the most important officer to the less important ones.

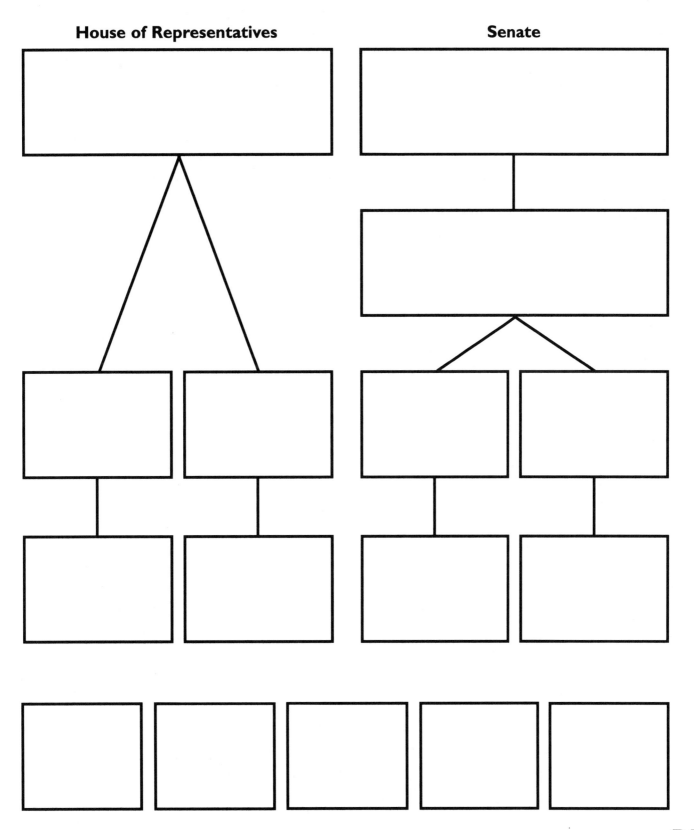

House of Representatives

Senate

Congressional Committees

Several thousand bills are introduced into Congress during a two-year term—so many bills that senators or representatives could not read all of them and still do the rest of their jobs. Therefore, Congress created **standing committees**, permanent committees in each house that deal with bills on subjects that must be considered every year. Once a bill is introduced, the leader of the house sends it to a committee that holds hearings and studies the bill.

Large committees have several **subcommittees** within them. These deal with specific issues that come under the larger subject of the standing committee. For instance, the Senate committee on Energy and Natural Resources might have subcommittees that specialize in fossil and synthetic fuels, and solar, wind, and geothermal energies.

There are other types of committees. **Select committees** deal with topics that are not covered by the standing committees. **Joint committees** include senators and representatives who work together to get bills through their houses. If both houses pass a bill but disagree on details, they form a **conference committee** to work out a compromise.

House of Representatives

Agriculture
Appropriations
Banking and Financial Services
Commerce
Government Reform and Oversight
International Relations
National Security
Science
Small Business
Standards of Official Conduct
Transportation and Infrastructure
Veterans' Affairs
Ways and Means

Senate

Agriculture, Nutrition and Forestry
Appropriations
Armed Services
Banking, Housing and Urban Affairs
Commerce, Science and Transportation
Energy and National Resources
Environment and Public Works
Finance
Foreign Relations
Labor and Human Resources
Rules and Administration
Small Business
Veterans' Affairs

Name _____

Join a Committee!

A. Below are listed several standing committees in the Senate. Beside each Senate committee, write the name of the House committee that is most like it.

1. Appropriations _____

2. Veterans' Affairs _____

3. Agriculture, Nutrition and Forestry _____

4. Rules and Administration _____

5. Banking, Housing and Urban Affairs _____

6. Foreign Relations _____

B. The main ideas of bills that senators might have introduced into their house are given below. Under each bill, write the name of the Senate committee that will study it.

1. A bill to increase the number of police officers in cities throughout the U.S.

   Committee: _____

2. A bill to raise minimum wage for all full-time employees.

   Committee: _____

3. A bill to increase the amount of money per depositor that is insured by the Federal Deposit Insurance Corporation.

   Committee: _____

4. A bill to create a national park on the California coast to protect rare sea life.

   Committee: _____

5. A bill that requires school lunches to include two servings of fruits or vegetables.

   Committee: _____

6. A trade agreement treaty between the United States and Mexico.

   Committee: _____

Lobbies and Political Action Committees

Most people have ideas about what the government should be doing for its citizens. As individuals, we can influence Congress and the President by voting for candidates who think as we do, by working in election campaigns, and by writing letters and e-mail to our elected officials. However, we can have an even greater effect on our government's decisions if we join together in large groups that work for the same cause. That is what lobbies and political action committees are all about.

A lobby is a special interest group. Such a group might be interested in changing the way health maintenance organizations (HMOs) treat their clients, in preventing Congress from putting restrictions on owning and using guns or in being able to join two large companies together. A lobby hires a person–a lobbyist–to communicate its point of view to Congress and to try to convince Congress to vote a certain way.

Political action committees (PACs) are a more recent development in politics. These organizations are the political branch of a special interest group. For instance, churches are not allowed to try to influence political decisions, but independent people with similar religious beliefs can form a PAC and work to change laws. PACs raise voluntary donations of money from people who agree with their cause. They give this money to election campaigns of people they support and to the political party that will work for their goals. PACs control large amounts of money. Recently, they contributed about $9 million to people running for office.* It is important to understand lobbies and PACs because they have great influence to change laws and our lives.

*Information adapted from *American Civics* by William S. Vincent and William H. Hartley, Holt, Rinehart and Winston, Austin 1996.

36

"PAC" Your Bags and Take Them to the Lobby of the Capitol!

A. Match the issue with the PAC or lobby that is most likely to support it.

_____ 1. American Association of Retired Persons

_____ 2. National Wildlife Federation

_____ 3. People for the Ethical Treatment of Animals

_____ 4. Consumer Confederation of America

_____ 5. National Association for the Advancement of Colored People

_____ 6. National Organization for Women

_____ 7. American Federation of Labor-Congress of Industrial Organizations

a. increase the number of African Americans who have jobs on television shows

b. discourage manufacturers from moving factories to countries with cheaper labor

c. reduce prices for medicine required for older people

d. an end to the testing of household chemicals and beauty products on animals

e. stricter laws against toys dangerous to children

f. protection of wolves in Yellowstone Park and several western states

g. equal pay for men and women doing similar jobs

B. Now apply your understanding of lobbying to your school. Below, list four positive changes that you would like to lobby your principal or school board to adopt.

1. _____

2. _____

3. _____

4. _____

Name _____

A Senator's Schedule

Senators have many jobs they do during their busy days. They serve on committees, vote in their house, have conferences with the President and with other members of Congress, solve problems for people back home and go home to keep in touch with the people who vote for them. Below are activities a senator might be doing during a single day. On the next page, you will fill in the senator's schedule.

1. Eats breakfast with the President, who tries to persuade her and other senators to vote for a bill he wants passed.

2. Attends a hearing of the Banking, Housing and Urban Affairs Committee.

3. Talks with other senators about the bill they are all sponsoring and decides what strategy is best for getting the bill passed.

4. Talks to the party whip to find out how many more votes the whip has raised for her bill.

5. Takes 15 minutes for a photo opportunity with a labor union official who helped the senator get elected.

6. Introduces a special bill for a person in her home state who should have been awarded a military medal 30 years ago, but who was not given the medal for political reasons.

7. Meets with two of her staff members who have research to give her about a bill that is coming up for a vote.

8. Attends a conference committee meeting to work out the differences between the Senate's version and the House's version of a bill that will shortly go to the President.

9. Gives a brief interview to a national television network about the bill she and other senators are sponsoring.

10. Confirms that the secretary has plane reservations for Friday so the senator can return to her home state to campaign for re-election.

11. Goes to a thousand-dollar-a-plate fund-raiser to help raise money from party supporters for the next election.

12. Reads newspapers and the briefings her staff have prepared on committee business.

13. Must attend a roll-call vote to override the President's veto of a bill.

38

Name _____

The Senator's Schedule for Tomorrow

You are a member of the senator's staff. The senator has asked you to prepare her daily schedules and to give her tomorrow's schedule at the end of today's work. You must use at least eight of the activities listed on page 38. You may add activities that you think of as long as they are real duties of a senator. Be realistic about how much time each activity will take, but know that two or more things can happen in one hour.

7:00 a.m.

8:00 a.m.

9:00 a.m.

10:00 a.m.

11:00 a.m.

12:00 p.m.

1:00 p.m.

2:00 p.m.

3:00 p.m.

4:00 p.m.

5:00 p.m.

6:00 p.m.

7:00 p.m.

Colorful Legislative Terms

Some words that describe what Congress does come from other occupations, historical situations or slang. Below are several unusual words and their definitions. Read the terms and their definitions to prepare for the exercise on the next page.

cave of the winds: This term is sometimes used to name the Senate because senators have the right to filibuster. A filibuster is a speech against a bill that goes on and on with either one senator speaking or a series of senators taking turns speaking.

Christmas tree bill: This type of bill has many extra, unrelated pieces of legislation added to it like decorations on a Christmas tree.

coattail: During a presidential election, a very popular President would help to elect members of Congress that come from his or her political party. The members of Congress are then said to have ridden into office on the President's coattails.

grass roots: Ordinary citizens who are not politicians are the grass roots of our nation. To say that something comes from a grass roots movement means that it is the people, not the legislators, who started the idea and who work to get it passed.

lame duck: A legislator who has been voted out of office and who is serving the last two months between the election and the swearing-in of the new legislator is called a lame duck. The term shows the defeated legislator's lack of power to get a bill passed.

logrolling: Originally this term described neighbors helping one another to clear their land for farming. After cutting down a tree, the neighbors would work as a group to roll the log to a place for burning. In Congress two or more senators would agree to help one another pass their bills. "You vote for my bill, and I'll vote for yours."

pork barrel bill: A bill that uses federal money for a special project in the legislator's home state or district is a pork barrel bill. For instance, Congress might pass a bill to build a dam in Colorado. This would bring money into the state, provide jobs for many workers and make the senator or representative who got it passed a very popular person. The term comes from the 1800s when the word *pork* was used as slang for government money spent on local projects. At that time, pork was preserved by keeping it in barrels of salt, so bills distributing money like this were called "pork barrel bills."

stumping: A legislator who is stumping is traveling around his or her home district making speeches. Originally, a speaker in rural districts would stand on a tree stump in order to be seen and heard by the crowd.

war chest: A war chest is the money the legislator has raised to finance his or her next election campaign.

Definitions adapted from *The Congress Dictionary* by Paul Dickson and Paul Clancy, New York, John Wiley & Sons, Inc., 1993 and from *The World Book Encyclopedia*, Chicago, World Book, Inc., 1990.

Name _____

Drawing Colorful Terms

Pick five terms from the glossary on page 40. Make a drawing for each term that shows the origin of the word and its political meaning.

Example: A carpetbagger is a person who moves from one state to get elected to an office in another state. After the Civil War, northern carpetbaggers moving to the south supposedly packed all their belongings in a type of suitcase made of carpet material. You might draw a picture of a person crossing the border from one state to another carrying a bag made of carpet material with the words *Smith for Senator* printed on it.

Word   **Drawing**

1. _____

2. _____

3. _____

4. _____

5. _____

Internet Research Ideas

1. It would be interesting to learn about senators or representatives who broke ground for different minority groups by gaining the highest seats in the government. Among the first Asian American Congresspersons were Hiram Fong, Daniel Inouye, Patsy Mink and Daniel Akaka. The first African Americans elected to Congress arrived during Reconstruction. Among these were Hiram Revels, Benjamin S. Turner, Josiah T. Walls and Robert Brown Elliott. Shirley Chisholm became the first African American woman to serve in the House in 1969. Charles Curtis was the first Native American elected to the House in 1892 and the first in the Senate in 1906. More recently, Ben Nighthorse Campbell of Colorado has also been elected to both houses. Hispanic Americans in Congress include Romualdo Pacheco in the 19th century and Dennis Chavez, Herman Badillo and Ilena Ros-Lehtinen in the 20th century.

2. Amendment 17 changed the way senators are elected. Find out about the old system of election, the Populist and Progressive parties that worked for the direct election of senators, the reasons why they believed this was more fair that the old method and how senators are currently elected.

3. Congress has the power to declare war, while the President as commander in chief of the military can send troops to places throughout the world. In 1964, Congress virtually gave up its power to declare war with the Gulf of Tonkin Resolution that gave President Johnson great powers to conduct the Vietnam Conflict. Study this example of checks and balances going wrong, and write arguments defending or opposing the actions of Congress and Johnson.

4. Students can do biographical research on senators and representatives, some of whom are listed below.

   a. "Czar" Joseph G. Cannon was a powerful Speaker of the House.

   b. Senator Robert F. Kennedy ran for the presidency in 1968 and was assassinated in June of that year while campaigning.

   c. Senator Joseph McCarthy was a key figure in creating the "red scare" in the early 1950s.

   d. Sam Rayburn served in the House of Representatives from 1937-1961; most of that time he was Speaker of the House.

   e. Strom Thurmond led the Dixiecrat revolt against the Democrats in 1948 and holds the record for the longest filibuster by a single person.

   f. John Quincy Adams served 17 years in the House of Representatives after his single term as U.S. President.

42

Internet Research Ideas

g. Senator Sam Ervin presided over the 1973 Senate Wat_____ Hearings, the investigation of President Nixon's crimes in the 1972 presidential election.

h. Senator Ted Kennedy (brother of John and Robert) can never run for President because of an automobile accident that killed a woman in the late 1960s.

i. Daniel Webster, Henry Clay and John C. Calhoun were the most influential members of Congress between the War of 1812 and the Civil War.

j. Thaddeus Stevens was the leader of the post-Civil War Radical Republicans.

k. Speaker of the House Newt Gingrich was swept into office on a tide of conservative votes and promised to fulfill the Contract with America.

l. Thomas "Tip" O'Neill was a highly respected Speaker of the House.

m. Robert "Fighting Bob" LaFollette, Sr., was a noted reformer during the Progressive age. He was almost nominated to run for President.

n. Hubert Humphrey, a liberal from Minnesota, ran for President in 1968.

o. Representative Jeannette Rankin voted against declaring war before World War I and World War II.

p. Senator George Norris of Nebraska has several laws named for him, and he worked nearly two decades to get the Tennessee Valley Authority into law.

q. Senator Barry Goldwater of Arizona ran for President in 1964 against President Lyndon Johnson. Johnson won by a landslide.

r. Representative Barbara Jordan served on the House Judiciary Committee that wrote and voted on the articles of impeachment against President Nixon.

s. Davy Crockett, one of the heroes of the Alamo, was a representative from Tennessee for three terms before he moved further west.

t. Senator John McCain of Arizona ran for the Republican nomination for President in 2000.

u. Shirley Chisholm ran for President in 1968; she was the first African American woman to run for that office.

v. Nicholas Longworth was Speaker of the House and married Theodore Roosevelt's eldest daughter Alice.

Internet Research Ideas

5. The Great Compromise reached in the Constitutional Convention resolved the debate between the large-state plan and the small-state plan. The large states wanted representation to be based on population. The smaller states wanted equal representation for all states in Congress. Find out how the Great Compromise solved this debate and what went on at the Constitutional Convention over this issue.

6. During Reconstruction (the period after the Civil War) the Radical Republicans controlled Congress and virtually controlled the nation by overriding President Andrew Jackson's vetoes and finally by impeaching him. Research the politics of this period, which was one of the few times that the checks and balances among the three branches of government did not work.

7. The congressional pages are an opportunity that middle school students can participate in directly. Pages deliver messages and run errands for senators and representatives. They must be in middle school to qualify and must be nominated by a Congressperson from their state. Do research on the pages and report to your class. You might apply to be nominated as a page if your parents think this is a good idea.

8. The special benefits that senators and representatives get beyond their salaries are called perquisites ("perks"). These include being able to mail letters about congressional business for free and having office space in one of the congressional buildings. Find out what other free or special privileges that members of Congress get with their jobs.

Multiple Intelligence Activities

Verbal/Linguistic Intelligence

1. Write a letter or e-mail to a senator or representative on an issue that concerns you.

2. Prepare for and conduct a Lincoln-Douglas debate (two students) or a regular debate (four students) on a current, controversial topic being considered in Congress.

3. Use computers to write and publish a House Journal based on the mock congress activity.

Visual/Spatial Intelligence

1. The British burned the Capitol building in 1814 during the War of 1812. Find pictures or designs of the original building. Pretend you are an architect hired to oversee the reconstruction of the Capitol. Draw the designs you would submit, showing how you would restore or change the building.

2. In Statuary Hall in the House of Representatives, each state has statues honoring its heroes. Choose a hero from your state and sketch, paint or sculpt that person with symbols showing his or her accomplishments.

3. Watch Jimmy Stewart in *Mr. Smith Goes to Washington*. This is useful for a view of the Senate chamber, an explanation of some of the Senate rules, an example of a committee hearing with witnesses and an example of a filibuster.

4. Make a poster showing how much political power each state has. Draw them from small to large based on the number of senators and representatives per state rather than on geographical size.

Auditory Intelligence

1. Students listen to famous speeches by senators and representatives with various purposes. The student could identify propaganda techniques, write down the major arguments of the speech, identify particularly strong or colorful words or expand his or her vocabulary with the help of a dictionary.

2. During a mock Congress, these students could be official recorders and write down the major arguments and votes as they occur.

Mathematical Intelligence

1. Research the raises in pay that senators and representatives have given themselves over the years. Make a chart or bar graph showing raises from 1789 to the present.

2. Find information on the internet about the current budget of the United States. Using major categories (such as military spending, Social Security payments, interest on the national debt and grants to education), create a pie chart or bar graph to show where the majority of our tax money is spent.

Kinesthetic Intelligence

1. In a mock Congress, kinesthetic learners could play the roles of pages or the Sergeant at Arms.

2. Students could review vocabulary in a game of charades. The kinesthetic learners act out the words. The student/team that guesses the word has to supply the definition to win points.

Multiple Intelligence Activities

Interpersonal Intelligence

1. Students with these skills would do well in a mock Congress as party whips, floor leaders, TV interviewers, the chair of a conference committee trying to reach a compromise on a bill or a Speaker.

2. To review for a test, these students could be leaders of study groups.

Intrapersonal Intelligence

1. Many men and women kept diaries when our country was founded, most notably James Madison, who provided important insights into the debates of the Constitutional Convention. Find books or internet sources of diaries by members of Congress. As you read, write your own thoughts about that person and the events of his or her life.

2. As you study Congress, make a personal scrapbook with such things as quotes from speeches that impressed you, pictures of members of Congress you admire, funny or dramatic stories about the legislature and ideas you would introduce into Congress if you could.

Multiple Intelligences

1. Senators and representatives can go on trips—called junkets—paid for by the government if they are investigating some issue Congress is considering. A group of students could work on this project together. Verbal/Linguistic: Read newspapers and newsmagazines investigating current trouble spots in the world and report back to the group. The group uses this information to decide where it wants to travel. Visual/Spatial: Draw a map and plot the route the group will take to that place. Interpersonal: Learn the customs and manners of the culture and teach the group correct behavior. Mathematical: Figure the budget for transportation, hotels, food, guides, etc. Linguistic: Learn some of the language and teach members of the group. Students of all intelligences could be involved. At the end of the "trip," students could report on the situation to a committee, design a travel brochure, videotape testimony on the situation, write newspaper articles or hold a debate on U.S. policy towards that place.

2. Students prepare for and hold a mock Congress. They could play roles such as party whip, legislator, set designer (to approximate a house chamber), research staff, Speaker, recorder, C-SPAN cameraman, etc., that would match the skills of students with each of the intelligences.

Answer Key

The Two Houses of Congress, page 9

1. Representative: two-year term; 25 years old; seven years a citizen; inhabitant of state that elected him.

   Senator: six-year term; 30 years old; nine years a citizen; inhabitant of state that elected him.

2. a. C; b. A; c. B; d. B; e. A; f. C; g. C; h. A; i. C; j. C

Methods of Passing Laws Outline, page 12

I. A bill is introduced into one of the houses (in this order):
   A. Bill is read by Clerk of the House.
   B. Bill is sent to committee.
   C. Committee sends bill to whole house.
   D. House debates the bill.
   E. First house passes the bill.

II. Bill goes to the other house to be voted on (in this order):
   A. Second house passes the bill.
   B. Bill goes to conference committee.

III. Bill is sent to President to sign (order of items does not matter):
   A. President signs the bill into law.
   B. President keeps the bill 10 days without signing it.
   C. Pocket veto occurs.
   D. President vetoes the bill.

IV. President returns the vetoed bill to Congress (order does not matter):
   A. Congress votes to override President's veto.
   B. Congress cannot get two-thirds vote to override veto.

Powers of Congress Worksheet, page 21

1. To coin money.
2. To regulate the value thereof (of money).
3. To regulate commerce with foreign nations.
4. To constitute tribunals (courts) inferior to the Supreme Court.
5. To exercise exclusive legislation, in all cases whatsoever, over (Washington, D.C.)
6. To declare war.
7. (To) grant letters of marque and reprisal.
8. To borrow money on the credit of the United States.

The Elastic Clause–Stretching the Powers of Congress, page 22

1. To regulate commerce . . . among the several states; or to establish . . . post roads.
2. To regulate commerce . . . among the several states.
3. To regulate commerce . . . among the several states.
4. To . . . provide for the . . . general welfare of the United States.
5. To . . . provide for the common defense. OR To make all laws which shall be necessary and proper for carrying into execution the foregoing powers.

Powers Forbidden to the Federal Government or to the States, page 26

Powers Forbidden to the Federal Government:

1. pay out money without appropriations laws

Powers Forbidden to the States:

1. coin money
2. emit bills of credit
3. keep armies and navies during peace
4. grant letters of marque and reprisal
5. fight a war
6. make laws that harm contracts
7. tax imports or exports except for inspections
8. enter foreign treaty or alliance
9. make a treaty or alliance with a state

Powers Forbidden to Both Federal and State Governments:

1. pass bills of attainder
2. pass *ex post facto* laws
3. grant titles of nobility
4. tax exports
5. suspend writ of *habeas corpus*

Thinking Skills: Classifying Vocabulary Words, page 27

A. Unfair Laws
   1. bill of attainder
   2. *ex post facto* laws
B. Types of Taxes
   1. capitation tax
   2. imposts or duties
   3. tonnage
C. Words That Name Income (Not Taxes) for a Person or Country
   1. revenue
   2. emolument
D. Words About Business or Trading Goods
   1. commerce
   2. receipts
   3. expenditures
E. Things That Require Counting People
   1. capitation tax
   2. enumeration

Separation of Powers, page 29

1. no
2. yes
3. yes
4. yes
5. yes
6. yes
7. yes
8. yes
9. yes
10. yes
11. yes

Answer Key

Checks and Balances,
page 31

1. yes
2. yes
3. no
4. yes
5. no
6. yes
7. yes
8. no
9. yes
10. no
11. yes
12. yes

Officers of the Senate and House of Representatives,
page 32

1. already given in text
2. party whips, important but of lower rank than the floor leaders
3. most important officer, Senate, Vice President of United States, President of the Senate
4. Senate, party whips, same duties and rank as those in the House
5. floor leader, majority leader, minority leader, rank above the party whips but are less powerful than the Speaker or President *Pro Tempore*
6. Senate, President *Pro Tempore*, second to the Vice President in importance
7. Senate, majority leader, minority leader, same rank as the House majority and minority leaders, but they are less important than the President *Pro Tempore* in their house.
8. Senators and representatives, head of a committee, most powerful committee leaders but less important than leaders responsible for gettings bills passed through Congress

Ranking Officers Chart,
page 33

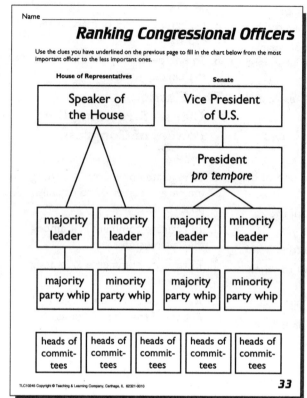

Join a Committee! page 35

A. 1. Appropriations
   2. Veterans' Affairs
   3. Agriculture
   4. Standards of Official Conduct
   5. Banking and Financial Services
   6. International Relations

B. 1. Banking, Housing and Urban Affairs
   2. Labor and Human Resources
   3. Banking, Housing and Urban Affairs
   4. Environment and Public Works
   5. Agriculture, Nutrition and Forestry
   6. Foreign Relations

"PAC" Your Bags and Take Them to the Lobby of the Capitol! page 37

A. 1. C
   2. F
   3. D
   4. E
   5. A
   6. G
   7. B